Preserving Your Next Generation

Alero Nwana

Copyright © 2020 by Alero Nwana

All rights reserved. No part of this publication may be reproduced, stored in any retrieval system, or transmitted in any form or by any means, for example through electronic, photocopy, recording without the prior written permission of the copyright owner.

ISBN:
    eBook: 978-1-7347424-0-4
    Paperback: 978-1-7347424-1-1

Printed in the United States of America.

Unless otherwise specified, all scripture quotations are taken from the New King James Version®. Copyright © 1982 by Thomas Nelson. Used by permission. All rights reserved.

Persons depicted in the stock imagery herein provided by stock.adobe.com are models. The said images are used for illustrative purposes only and cannot be copied or reused in any format outside of this publication.

Contents

Foreword..1

Credits..4

Prologue...7

1. Legacy: When and Where to Begin..........19
2. Raising your children – Glimpses from the Bible..29
3. Choosing a Spouse? Deep Thoughts.........49
4. Guide your Heavenly Treasures.................57
5. Could it Have Had a Different Ending?.....77
6. Make your Arrows Sharp............................95
7. Reflections..107
8. Bringing it Closer......................................115

Epilogue...121

Foreword

Alero Nwana, the author of the book, *Preserving Your Next Generation*, is a very resourceful person with a great passion for working with children. She has a natural flair for teaching the Bible to children and leading them in many Christian activities. This, together with the grace of God upon her life, made her a great asset to the Children's ministry of our church over the past thirty years. She would spend many hours writing and rehearsing the church's annual Easter and Christmas musicals for presentation by the children. It should be stated that what she did in and for the church had its origin in her own home, as she brought up her own children.

Preserving Your Next Generation is a great help to parents and would-be parents.

Parenting can be a very difficult task. It is also one which is much neglected among those blessed with children (biological or adopted) in our world today. For some, the neglect is as a result of not knowing how to go about it. There is no formal school for training parents, and some of those who fail as parents may not have been appropriately parented by anyone.

Whatever may be the cause of the neglect, failure to properly parent our children is the root of most societal ills that educational institutions and law enforcement agencies are grappling with in every nation of the world.

If any society will be rid of these ills, parents must be open to learn all that they can about biblical parenting and put these into practice in their families. One sure aid in this process is the work of this author.

In a very easy-to-read format, the author deals with parenting from the perspective of the Bible and her own personal experience of bringing up two sons who are making positive contributions to the society as adults today.

Knowing that no one can make a success of parenting without the help of God, the author provides opportunities for seeking the face of God in prayer throughout the book.

It is my prayer that God will use this book to enlighten, encourage, and strengthen the hands of those called by Him to bring up the next generation of nation-builders in Jesus' name. Amen.

Rev. Dr. Kayode Ilupeju
Pastor, Good News Baptist Church,
Surulere, Lagos. Nigeria

CREDITS

I dedicate this book to all the children that God brought my way through the children's ministry of Good News Baptist Church, Lagos, Nigeria. God used my interaction with children over the past 30 years to bring out the treasures I would never have known He put inside me. To all those children (a lot of them, now adults with their own families), thank you for helping me discover who God made me and for putting up with "Aunty Alero style." You wrote this book long before I penned a word. The times I spent with you in the classroom and preparing for various concerts were the happiest and most comforting of my life. God used those times to begin the process of putting me together. You all have been a huge blessing to me. Thank you.

To my biological children, watching you grow into God-fearing young men is a testimony to the truth and spirit of Proverbs 22:6: "train up a child the way he should go, when he is old, he will not depart from it." God used all the "in-between episodes" we had to refine our characters and bring out the love and deep affection we have for each other. You must pass it on...

To my grandchildren, I love you so much. I believe that you and my other grandchildren coming are my second chance from God! You are all arrows God has put in my hands, and I am deeply grateful to Him.

To my dear husband, Endy, I appreciate your loving care and support since 1980.

To my pastor, Rev. (Dr.) Kayode Ilupeju, thank you for giving me the opportunity to serve and express God's gift at the time it mattered most. God never makes mistakes; His timings are perfect.

To all my close family and friends who have always been there for me, urging me on, thank you from the depth of my soul.

To my dear sister, Rita, who helped in editing this book, I am deeply grateful.

Thank you to my readers for opening the pages of this book. You are the parents of *the next generation of children* with hearts ready to partner with God in preserving a generation of boys, girls, men and women set apart to transform this world.

To my heavenly father, the Alpha and Omega, I openly and gladly say without you my life would have had no meaning. Thank you for redeeming me through the death and resurrection of your son, Jesus Christ my Savior and Lord. I ascribe to you alone, all glory and honour for being long suffering with me and making sure I did not stray from your presence. Thank you for teaching me obedience through the things I suffered.

Prologue

What legacy do you as a parent or guardian, plan on leaving for your children? Have you thought about it? This question bothered me for many years. My first thought was centered around material possessions and a good education. Then again, I wondered: "Could that be all?" When I considered the insignificant material possession I have to leave to my children, I became unsettled. The Bible clearly says, "a good man leaves an inheritance for his children and children's children..." (Proverbs 13:22). So again, I thought: "Is God talking about material inheritance?"

I have made some wrong decisions with far-reaching consequences trying to figure things out on my own. I have been driven to the feet of the Father, God Almighty, and my journey in learning to wait on the LORD for specific answers is the focus of this book. I thank the LORD for providing answers to my numerous questions, correcting me and showing me the way in my various quests.

One of my favorite scriptures is Psalm 34:4: "I sought the Lord and he answered me; he delivered me from all my fears" (NIV). I knew I had to seek God, so I started a conversation with Him on the type of inheritance He meant for me to leave my children and the process I should follow. God did deliver me from my many mix-ups and fears. In that process, He spoke to me on the type of responsibility the scripture imposes on me, and I dare say, on every parent. God took me through some experiences in my marriage and career to point me to what He really expected of me. I didn't get it at those times.

God never runs out of patience. He is longsuffering, so He did what any loving and caring parent would do to get my attention. He did not allow me to just get on any road, and when I insisted, He stopped me from being too comfortable within a path He had not chosen for me. What I now know to be God's divine interruptions were actually very painful experiences at the time. But God waited, took care of me, and comforted me. He brought me to a point where I finally could see the road ahead. I discerned His firm but loving voice saying, "the experiences you have had, the winding roads, the ups and downs, the betrayals, mountaintop and valley experiences, were planned and permitted by me to build treasures within you worth passing on. These and not mere worldly possessions are what I want you to leave and pass on as an inheritance."

It took some time for me to get a deeper understanding of what God was saying. I examined another one of my favorite scriptures, Psalm 71:18b (NIV): "…. till I declare **your power** to the next generation, **your mighty acts** to all who are to come." I turn to this scripture in challenging seasons for assurance of God's presence. It is God's word and confirmation that I will live a long life. Surely, I will! Given this fact, I feel I must be prepared to teach His word, especially as it pertains to children. I recited and prayed Psalm 71:18b for reassurance that I would live through every trying situation because I had not yet begun the assignment God had committed into my hands.

But I later realized that this was not the only reason God led me to Psalm 71:18b. The other scriptures the Holy Spirit led me to study provided a clearer understanding:

Exodus 10:2(a) NKJV "and that you tell in the hearing of your son and your son's son the mighty things which I have done."

Exodus 12:26-27(a) NKJV: "And it shall be, when your children say to you, 'What do you mean by this service?' that you shall say, 'It is the Passover sacrifice of the LORD, who passed over the houses of the children of Israel in Egypt when He struck the Egyptians and delivered our households."

Deuteronomy 11:19 NKJV "You shall teach them to your children, speaking of them when you sit in your house, when you walk by the way, when you lie down and when you rise up."

Joel 1:3 NKJV "Tell your children about it, let your children tell their children, And their children another generation."

The insight from these scriptures provided a better understanding of my assignment. God was asking me to nudge all parents, and let them know, not what they didn't already know but the urgency thereof. The current generation of children needs to be equipped by their parents to "rescue" coming generations from messages and lifestyles designed to alter God's plan for mankind. They need to know that God's expectations of His people in Bible days are still the same today and will never change. It is therefore, vitally important that parents are able to provide contextual and historically accurate answers to our children's questions about the things of God. In addition, we need to let our children know how big a deal the mighty power of God is so they too can come to know Him through His mighty works in contemporary times.

It is my hope and prayer that this book,

Preserving Your Next Generation

Preserving Your Next Generation, will help parents ensure that we preserve the faith God has called us into. Our children and generations yet unborn need to know what God has done in our lives, and the deliverances and victories He gave to us. Most importantly, our children need to hear about our salvation, the heart of God's love shown to us through the gift of His Son, Jesus the Christ. We need to let them see and read God's word in our everyday conscious and unconscious decisions and actions. What we tell our children about God's standards and expectations must match what we do.

Children are the vessels that God has provided to ensure that the truth and power of God's word in the scripture are preserved. The legacy God has called us to leave our children involves equipping and intentionally evangelizing them at an early age as soon as they can discern and understand.

What then do we need to let them know?

- How to discern the voice of God.
- How loving, powerful and awesome God is

so that they learn to avoid the mistakes we made.
- How to pray, worship and tell others about God (and bring others into God's family).
- How to understand God's great love, mercy and grace.
- How to understand that there is power and life in God's word.
- How to know that there is life in the Blood of Jesus the Christ.
- How to follow God in true obedience.
- How to detect the voice and schemes of the devil, the liar and father of all lies.
- How to serve God from an early age.
- How to study and memorize scripture.

These are some of the most important things we need to impress on our children in preparing and equipping them to follow the footsteps of Jesus as they grow and mature.

It is our role as parents to teach our children to put on the full armor of God so they can stand against the enemy's schemes, and to remember the great sacrifice of Jesus Christ on the cross.

We must pass on and pass down the "traditions" of God's family such as loving those who hate us, observing the Lord's Supper, living in humility, giving back to God for what He gave to us and so on.

These godly traditions may initially appear to be a lot for us to pass on to our children. However, with prayers and intentional parenting skills, we can succeed. I pray we all do.

Apart from all of these, our lifestyle is the living manual that our children will treasure most when we are gone. It will not be our bank accounts or the real estate we leave behind. Our present-day homes are where we begin to write our "living will and testament" in the hearts of our children. It is not in a law office. *(No offence to parents that are lawyers, being one myself)*. Preparing the next generation to really know, love and serve God truly begins with us.

I invite you to explore this exciting route with me. Let us start …

PRAYER SEED:

Holy Spirit equip me for this exciting but serious journey in preparing my legacy for my children. I need your strength and wisdom.

I need patience and your love to reach my children with God's precious instructions. Help me not to let God down. Walk with us every step of the way and give my children's hearts to God. Amen

SCRIPTURE BOOST:

> "I have strength for all things in Christ Who empowers me [I am ready for anything and equal to anything through Him Who infuses inner strength into me; I am self-sufficient in Christ's sufficiency]."
> Philippians 4:13 AMPC

> "We will not hide them from their children, Telling to the generation to come the praises of the LORD, And His strength and His wonderful works that He has done."
> Psalms 78:4 NKJV

My Action Journal

I will begin with God's help to:

1.

2.

3.

"The success of your child's journey in life is not only in God's hands but in yours as well".

AleroN

1/One

Legacy: When and Where to Begin

The womb

What has the womb got to do with legacy? Actually, that is the beginning! The journey of a man starts in the womb. Afterall, that is where God started His love and Father-child relationship with us. Let us look at scriptural evidence.

> "Listen, O coastlands, to Me, And take heed, you peoples from afar! The LORD has called Me from the womb; From the matrix of My mother He has made mention of My name.
>
> "And now the LORD says, Who formed

Me from the womb to be His Servant, To bring Jacob back to Him, So that Israel is gathered to Him (For I shall be glorious in the eyes of the LORD, And My God shall be My strength."
Isaiah 49:1, 5 NKJV

Isaiah heard God tell him his assignment from his mother's womb. There is activity with the divine and also with humanity right from the beginning. We can be a part of what God is doing by preparing our minds and cooperating with God in laying the foundations for a sound and godly heritage for our children.

The case of Elizabeth

Elizabeth, the mother of John the Baptist and Mary, the mother of Jesus Christ, were cousins. Mary had gone to visit Elizabeth shortly after her encounter with the Angel Gabriel. The baby incubating and developing in Elizabeth's womb leapt for joy when he heard Mary and Elizabeth exchange greetings. This response was felt by Elizabeth in her physical body though we know it originated in the spirit realm. Divine power and supernatural intervention were at play. Jesus and John were both conceived by divine intervention and the power of the Holy Spirit. Both had the "DNA of the Holy Spirit" and could, therefore, relate in spirit-led ways. (Luke 1:15b) It is also a known biological phenomenon and confirmed by scriptures that babies respond to sound while they are developing and being formed in the womb. (Luke 1:41).

Parents, we need to ask ourselves whose voices or sounds we want ingrained in the DNA of our children. Whose voice do we want them to intuitively recognize and respond to? The answer to this question is entirely up to us.

I feel led by God to encourage parents – particularly expectant mothers, to be careful where they go, what they read, and to be sensitive with songs they listen to during the nine months they incubate God's gift. This is a very delicate stage in the development of babies and a lot can go wrong with the destinies of children if parents are careless. Physical and spiritual sensitivity and discernment are desirable. The womb is where child evangelism should start. If you treat your womb as a place to teach unborn children the voice of God, then when they are born, they will intuitively gravitate towards the voice of God. If this is followed up by introducing children early to environments where the word of God and worship are reinforced (primarily your home and later the church), by faith, such children will commit their lives to Christ at an early age with a good understanding of what they are doing.

> *"To him the doorkeeper opens, and the sheep hear his voice; and he calls his own sheep by name and leads them out. And when he brings out his own sheep, he goes before them;* **and the sheep follow him, for they know his voice.** *Yet they will by no means follow a stranger, but will flee from him, for they do not know the voice of strangers."*
> John 10:3-5 NJKV

The Home

In your home, teach your children to pray and read the Bible. Let your children see you read the Bible and pray consistently. Pray with them and for them. Teach them how to pray and tell them why they need to pray. Let prayer become their second instinct. Involve children in family Bible reading as soon as they can read. Before then, read to them and engage them in age-appropriate memorization of simple Bible verses. Children love challenges. When they are positively challenged, they have a better propensity to handle and solve problems as they grow.

When children learn to crawl and walk, they face numerous challenges that they need to overcome. In order to grow, they need to overcome the fear of falling, fear of being trampled by adults, fear of falling off a bed, and so on. A 1-year-old child has his own peculiar challenges to grapple with. Even at this delicate and formative stage, babies and toddlers can be taught to call on the name of Jesus. Just by saying "Jesus" or "*Jesus can help you better than I can*" is enough to keep whispering into their ears. Children can recognize the name Jesus, God, and Holy Spirit very early in their development. *At about age* two, children can be taught simple Bible verses such as Psalm 23:1 "The Lord is my Shepard I shall not want", "God is love" (1John 4:16b) and "God loves me." (John 3:16a)

Remember, it is from the womb that prayers for unborn children begin. This should continue in the home when they are born and as they grow up. These are the savings we make towards our legacy and their inheritance.

It is also God's desire for us to raise our children to know and obey Him. This is what God said concerning Abraham:

> "For I have known him, in order that he may **command his children and his household after him,** that they keep the way of the LORD, to do righteousness and justice, that the LORD may bring to Abraham what He has spoken to him."
> Genesis 18:19 NKJV

God promised Abraham that he would make his name great, and Abraham would be a blessing. One way of receiving God's promises and blessings is by training our children to love and obey God. God rewarded Abraham's obedience. In addition to becoming extremely wealthy, Abraham became and is still a reference point for a true and meaningful blessing.

Prayer Seed

Father, I recognise that my child is a gift to me from you. I ask for help in raising him/her to know and recognise your voice at an early age. Help me to be alive to this responsibility so that the evil one will not gain a foothold into his/her life.

I silence every strange voice speaking over my children. May my children never respond to strange voices but to the voice of Jesus Christ the Good Shepherd. In Jesus mighty name, Amen.

Scripture Boost:

"Train up a child in the way he should go, and when he is old he will not depart from it."
Proverbs 22:6 NKJV

"My sheep hear My voice, and I know them, and they follow Me. And I give them eternal life, and they shall never perish; neither shall anyone snatch them out of My hand."
John 10:27-28 NKJV

My Action Journal

I will begin with God's help to:

1.

2.

3.

2/Two

Raising your children – Glimpses from the Bible

There are many effective parenting examples in the Bible. We will sift through some of them. The strengths, weaknesses, successes and failures of these biblical parents provide strategies we can learn from and adopt in raising children today.

Elizabeth and Mary: Be Circumspect

Be circumspect in the choice of words you use when speaking to or about your children. Words are powerful. They can either be creative or destructive. Through your words you can encourage or discourage your children. So you need to carefully choose the words you use when speaking to or about your children. Also, guard important information about them and do not share without proper consideration. Information shared carelessly could interfere with their destinies.

"The tongue of the wise uses knowledge rightly" Proverbs 15:2a NKJV

Elizabeth and Mary are biblical examples of parents who chose their words and their audience carefully. We will see how their choices and responses impacted the lives of their children and ultimately impacted the legacy they left them.

Elizabeth hid her pregnancy from everyone for five months. I still wonder how she pulled that off…….. No one knew she was pregnant (except her husband … of course) and her cousin Mary to whom the Angel Gabriel had revealed the fact. In my opinion, God must have shut the mouth of Zachariah for over nine months so he wouldn't distort his son's destiny by his unbelief and utterances.

> *"But behold, you will be mute and not able to speak until the day these things take place, because you did not believe my words which will be fulfilled in their own time."*
> Luke 1:20 NKJV

Zachariah was only able to speak after the birth of his son to confirm that the baby's name was John, the name God had given him to which his destiny was tied. Words spoken about John were heavily guarded by his mother and by God's divine protection.

As parents, we also need to carefully choose our audience. Do not share everything God reveals to you about your children with everyone. In other words, be circumspect and intentional.

Mary was also very circumspect. The only person she visited and interacted with during her pregnancy, as recorded in the Bible, was Elizabeth, her cousin. She stayed with her for a period of 3 months, mindful of Angel Gabriel's revelation about Jesus. It is recorded that Mary kept all of God's revelation of the destiny and mission of her unborn child in her heart. She neither confided in nor sought prayer support from anyone.

> *"But Mary kept all these things and pondered them in her heart."*
> *Luke 2:19 NKJV*

In addition, Mary followed her son's ministry intently. She precipitated Jesus' first miracle of turning water into wine at the wedding in Cana of Galilee.

> *"On the third day there was a wedding in Cana of Galilee, and the mother of Jesus was there. Now both Jesus and His disciples were invited to the wedding. And when they ran out of wine, the mother of Jesus said to Him, "They have no wine." Jesus said to her, "Woman, what does your concern have to do with Me? My hour has not yet come." His mother said to the servants, "Whatever He says to you, do it." Now there were set there six waterpots of stone, according to the manner of purification of the Jews, containing twenty or thirty gallons apiece. Jesus said to them,*

"Fill the waterpots with water." And they filled them up to the brim. And He said to them, "Draw some out now, and take it to the master of the feast." And they took it. When the master of the feast had tasted the water that was made wine, and did not know where it came from (but the servants who had drawn the water knew), the master of the feast called the bridegroom."
John 2:1-9 NKJV

I have come to regard Mary as a mother who was given to prayer. It is my belief that she prayed and prepared Jesus for his ministry. She acknowledged her son's giftings and respected him in his role as Messiah. She even followed him to the Cross. While standing and watching in agony at her son hanging between two criminals, she may even have remembered Simeon's prophecy saying "...a sword shall pierce your heart" spoken during Jesus dedication thirty years earlier. *(Luke 2:35)*. She must have known and accepted at that point that he was fulfilling God's purpose for his life.

Do you honour your children's personalities and their career/ministry choices? Do you prayerfully seek God's purpose and His will for your children? Failure to do so can leave your children vulnerable and may create a dent on the legacy you leave them.

Lois and Eunice: Faith Legacy Through Teaching

Timothy's grandmother and mother were godly women who raised and prayed Timothy into his destiny. They taught him the scriptures from an early age, which made him wise for salvation. Apostle Paul had this to say about Timothy's Christian upbringing:

> "...and how from childhood you have known the Holy Scriptures, which are able to make you wise for salvation through faith which is in Christ Jesus."
> II Timothy 3:15 NKJV

Lois and Eunice both lived a faith-filled life that young Timothy saw and was able to emulate as he grew into a young adult. They are examples of intentional parenting backed up with exemplary living. Are you doing the same?

"when I call to remembrance the genuine faith that is in you, which dwelt first in your grandmother Lois and your mother Eunice, and I am persuaded is in you also."
II Timothy 1:5 NKJV

We see a trail of faith living here. Timothy was the third generation of a faith-filled family. As Timothy grew up, he was able to make the right choices in following God. He became a dedicated follower and an "adopted Son" of Paul. He was also a great asset to the other apostles in the early Church as they all worked hard towards the spread of the gospel. What a legacy!

There should be no room for carelessness in matters regarding the future of our children. God took the time to plan their future before implanting them in the womb. God is a perfect God, and He makes no mistakes. He is very intentional, and even in our mistakes, His divine mercy works to achieve His purposes.

Let us see what happened in the case of Rebecca, Isaac's wife.

Rebecca: Do not be Manipulative

Rebecca, the mother of Esau and Jacob, was shown to be manipulative by her actions. Rebecca instigated and masterminded the deceit that caused her husband Isaac to mistakenly give the family's generational blessing to his son Jacob instead of Esau his older twin brother, as was the custom. Why would she do such a devious thing?

According to scriptures, Esau married wives from a foreign nation that caused grief to both Rebecca and her husband.

> "When Esau was forty years old, he took as wives Judith the daughter of Beeri the Hittite, and Basemath the daughter of Elon the Hittite. And they were a grief of mind to Isaac and Rebekah."
> Genesis 26:34-35 NKJV

Here is my own theory of why Rebecca did what she did. She must have nursed a deep-seated resentment for her daughters in-law and could not imagine those wives enjoying the "family blessing." Mothers in-law must learn not to be spiteful but forgiving and accommodating. Being unforgiving and spiteful is a sure way of planting bad seeds into the future of our children and leaving a legacy of hatred, bitterness and strife.

Rebecca may also have thought that since God told her that the older of her twin sons would serve the younger, then it was her place to make it happen. Parents cannot orchestrate their children's destinies themselves. Attempting to do this will only delay God's plans or totally mislead our children. We ought to pray our children into fulfilling their destinies. However, Rebecca took matters into her own hands and ended up adding more confusion to her already chaotic household.

"Now it came to pass, when Isaac was old and his eyes were so dim that he could not see, that he called Esau his older son and said to him, "My son." And he answered him, "Here I am." Then he said, "Behold now, I am old. I do not know the day of my death. Now therefore, please take your weapons, your quiver and your bow,

and go out to the field and hunt game for me. And make me savory food, such as I love, and bring it to me that I may eat, that my soul may bless you before I die." Now Rebekah was listening when Isaac spoke to Esau his son. And Esau went to the field to hunt game and to bring it. So Rebekah spoke to Jacob her son, saying, "Indeed I heard your father speak to Esau your brother, saying, 'Bring me game and make savory food for me, that I may eat it and bless you in the presence of the LORD before my death.' Now therefore, my son, obey my voice according to what I command you. Go now to the flock and bring me from there two choice kids of the goats, and I will make savory food from them for your father, such as he loves. Then you shall take it to your father, that he may eat it, and that he may bless you before his death."
Genesis 27:1-10 NKJV

What high-level scheming at play! The outcome may have been different had Rebecca taken time to pray and ask God for help with her emotions and family life. She sowed a seed of discord between her sons. The result was disastrous for the entire family. The parents "lost" their two children to unnecessary sojourns, distortion and delay in the fulfilment of their destinies. The two brothers were estranged for life and lived in mutual distrust of and fear for each other. Jacob literally became a slave worker in his uncle Laban's business for many years. Laban dealt him the same blow he and his mother dealt Esau. Thanks to God's divine mercy and grace, his destiny was restored. We can't say the same for Esau, who became the father of those who still fight believers today.

I believe it would have been easier for Jacob to find fulfillment had his mother been positively responsive to God's prophesy regarding her children. Her manipulative behavior wrecked the entire family, and she lost the opportunity God gave her to be a destiny-helper to her children. As parents, we cannot manipulate our children into fulfilling God's purpose for their lives. What is needed is prayer and a determination to do God's will in our own lives.

Mrs. Zebedee: Be Audacious in Praying for Your Children

Mrs. Zebedee is a parent after my own heart! She was bold and understood how to handle matters of destiny. Unlike Rebecca, she was not manipulative but understood that some issues are best handled at the source. She was not about to let the determination of her children's destiny slide past. Not on her watch! Towards the end of Jesus ministry, while he was preparing for the Cross, (it was not recorded in the Bible that she knew this fact, but we do) she took her two grown children to Jesus and made an audacious request but with an attitude of utmost reverence:

> "Then the mother of Zebedee's sons came to Him with her sons, kneeling down and asking something from Him. And He said to her, "What do you wish?" She said to Him, "Grant that these two sons of mine may sit, one on Your right hand and the other on the left, in Your kingdom." But Jesus answered and said, "You do not know what you ask. Are you able to drink the cup that I am about to drink, and be baptized with the

baptism that I am baptized with?" They said to Him, "We are able." So He said to them, "You will indeed drink My cup, and be baptized with the baptism that I am baptized with; but to sit on My right hand and on My left is not Mine to give, but it is for those for whom it is prepared by My Father."
Matthew 20:20-23 NKJV

Although Jesus could not give her what she requested the way she had prayed, she got Jesus and her sons into a conversation that resulted in the affirmation that they would partake of Jesus suffering (which by the way is what all believers are called into). But more than this, we see from scriptures that her sons' position as part of Jesus "inner circle" remained strong. Jesus chose the Zebedee brothers, James and John, along with Peter, out of His twelve disciples to have the singular privilege of being the ones to witness His agony and to watch with Him as He prepared to fulfil His own destiny to save mankind from the power of sin and death.

"And He took with Him Peter and the two sons of Zebedee, and He began to be sorrowful and deeply distressed. Then He said to them, "My soul is exceedingly sorrowful, even to death. Stay here and watch with Me."
Matthew 26:37-38

What deep intimacy Jesus displayed here! My question to you dear parent is how bold are you when you pray for your children? Do you present critical issues of their destinies to the only one who can say yes or no? Can you stand by whatever God says, knowing that His decisions over your children can never be wrong?

As parents, we are encouraged by the story of Mrs. Zebedee to be reverently audacious when praying for our children. We sow seeds of heaven's attestation and attention into their futures when we do this.

John, one of the sons of Mrs. Zebedee, ended up writing the gospel of John, the 3 letters of John, and probably the Book of Revelation when he was banished on the Island of Patmos.

"The Revelation of Jesus Christ, which God gave Him to show His servants things which must shortly take place. And He sent and signified it by His angel to His servant John, who bore witness to the word of God, and to the testimony of Jesus Christ, to all things that he saw. I, John, both your brother and companion in the tribulation and kingdom and patience of Jesus Christ, was on the island that is called Patmos for the word of God and for the testimony of Jesus Christ." Revelation 1:1-2, 9 NKJV

BATHSHEBA: BE WATCHFUL AND PROACTIVE

Bathsheba, one of King David's wives, was very insightful and watchful. King David promised that their son Solomon would be king after him. However, her stepson Adonijah usurped the throne with the backing of two of David's cabinet members. Bathsheba, upon hearing what Adonijah had done wasted no time in taking up the matter with David. She was not slothful, and she did not procrastinate. She acted in the heat of the moment and got results. That same day, David had Nathan the Priest anoint Solomon as King. That same day!

Preserving Your Next Generation

Dear parents, do you waste time moaning and complaining when things appear not to be going as planned or when "life just happens" to your children? Bathsheba's prompt intervention of bringing the matter to David's attention ensured that the destiny of her son was preserved.

As we can see from Bathsheba's example, timely parental intercession is required to give your children the homerun they need to win some of life's battles against God's plan for their lives. Some of these battles can be tough for them to handle on their own, even as grownups. God answers our prayers concerning our children when they align with His purpose for their lives.

"So Bathsheba went into the chamber to the king. (Now the king was very old, and Abishag the Shunammite was serving the king.) And Bathsheba bowed and did homage to the king. Then the king said, "What is your wish?" Then she said to him, "My lord, you swore by the LORD your God to your maidservant, saying, 'Assuredly

Solomon your son shall reign after me, and he shall sit on my throne.' So now, look! Adonijah has become king; and now, my lord the king, you do not know about it. He has sacrificed oxen and fattened cattle and sheep in abundance, and has invited all the sons of the king, Abiathar the priest, and Joab the commander of the army; but Solomon your servant he has not invited. And as for you, my lord, O king, the eyes of all Israel are on you, that you should tell them who will sit on the throne of my lord the king after him. Otherwise it will happen, when my lord the king rests with his fathers, that I and my son Solomon will be counted as offenders." And just then, while she was still talking with the king, Nathan the prophet also came in. So they told the king, saying, "Here is Nathan the prophet." And when he came in before the king, he bowed down before the king with his face to the ground. And Nathan said, "My lord, O king, have you said, 'Adonijah shall reign after me, and he shall sit on my throne'? For he has gone down today, and has sacrificed oxen and

fattened cattle and sheep in abundance, and has invited all the king's sons, and the commanders of the army, and Abiathar the priest; and look! They are eating and drinking before him; and they say, "Long live King Adonijah!' But he has not invited me your servant nor Zadok the priest, nor Benaiah the son of Jehoiada, nor your servant Solomon. Has this thing been done by my lord the king, and you have not told your servant who should sit on the throne of my lord the king after him?" …..just as I swore to you by the LORD God of Israel, saying, 'Assuredly Solomon your son shall be king after me, and he shall sit on my throne in my place,' so I certainly will do this day."
I Kings 1:15-27, 30 NKJV

Solomon's life and kingship were preserved through the timely intervention of a proactive mother who knew when, how and to whom her case should be presented. Are you like her?

Prayer Seed

Dear God, I acknowledge that I cannot train the children you have given me in my own power and wisdom. I need your help. Please help me as a parent to overcome whatever personal weaknesses I may have. Give me the virtues needed to give them a godly upbringing. If I have made mistakes in the past, please forgive me and do not let my children suffer for my wrong actions. Give me a second chance. I receive all the strength I need to nurture and sharpen my arrows. In Jesus name, Amen.

Scripture Boost

> "Behold, children are a heritage from the LORD, The fruit of the womb is a reward. Like arrows in the hand of a warrior, So are the children of one's youth. Happy is the man who has his quiver full of them; They shall not be ashamed but shall speak with their enemies in the gate."
> Psalms 127:3-5 NKJV

My Action Journal

I will begin with God's help to:

1.

2.

3.

3/Three

Choosing a Spouse? Deep Thoughts

You may be thinking about what the choice of a spouse has to do with intentional parenting. The two are deeply connected. The background, beliefs and general values of your spouse matter a lot. They impact the behaviors and lifestyle that will be adopted, tolerated and accepted in training your children as well as their character formation to a large extent. God as a loving parent has warned us not to be "unequally yoked" in marriage (and in all our relationships, including career, business, friendships and so on). We sometimes take this warning lightly to our own peril. Let us look at this scripture passage below in respect of marital choice.

> "Now **the son of an Israelite woman**, whose father was an Egyptian, went out among the children of Israel; and this **Israelite woman's son** and a man of Israel fought each other in the camp. And **the Israelite woman's son** blasphemed the name of the LORD and cursed; and so they brought him to Moses. (His mother's name was Shelomith the daughter of Dibri, of the tribe of Dan.) Then they put him in custody that the mind of the LORD might be shown to them. And the LORD spoke to Moses, saying, "Take outside the camp him who has cursed; then let all who heard him lay their hands on his head, and let all the congregation stone him. "Then you shall speak to the children of Israel, saying: 'Whoever curses his God shall bear his sin. And whoever blasphemes the name of the LORD shall surely be put to death. All the congregation shall certainly stone him, the stranger as well as him who is born in the land. When he blasphemes the name

of the LORD, he shall be put to death."
Leviticus 24:10-16 NKJV

The phrase "the son of an Israelite woman" was used three times in the short reference to point out that the son had little value for and understanding of the laws of God given to the Israelites, having been fathered by an Egyptian. As a result, he was not regarded and accepted as an Israelite.

The above passage shows that there can be consequences if parents do not share the same moral, ethical or biblical values. The essence of this book is not about marriage but raising godly children and leaving them a godly heritage. However, making the wrong choice in who you marry can have far-reaching consequences for your children. The Israelite woman's son, for example, ended up being stoned to death because he cursed the name of the Lord. He was a classic example of an ill-mannered child. Differences in his parents' belief system (Jewish and Egyptian), suggest that there may have been differences in parenting values and in the boundaries set in his home as well. You cannot give what you do not have.

Dear reader, please ponder on this issue very deeply and ask the Holy Spirit to counsel you on the principles you need to learn about being *"unequally yoked"* in terms of marital and other life-impacting choices.

Deep thoughts in choosing your spouse.
Deep fervent and earnest prayers to God.
Deep dependence on God in obedience.
Are foundational steps towards a godly legacy.

   AleroN

Prayer Seed

Father give me the wisdom I need to make the right decisions, especially on fundamental issues of my life. May my decisions be made with eternity in view. In Jesus name I pray, Amen.

Scripture Boost

"Do not be unequally yoked together with unbelievers. For what fellowship has righteousness with lawlessness? And what communion has light with darkness?"
II Corinthians 6:14 NKJV

My Action Journal

I will begin with God's help to:

1.

2.

3.

4/Four

Guide your Heavenly Treasures

Our children are part of the treasures God wants us to store up in heaven, where nothing can destroy them and where they are safe and complete. We must strive to build a spiritual safety nest all around them. The enemy is fighting tooth and nail to take control of their minds through many sophisticated and seemingly harmless tools. One of the most effective of these tools today is social media. Parents must also become social media savvy.

Being a Sunday schoolteacher, I interact closely with a lot of children and I noticed that my pre-teens and teenagers in church begin to get secretive as they strive for their own independence. I noticed the same attitude in my own children when they were that age. At this formative and important age range, our children become more curious about life and are not always as judicious in their choices as we would like them to be. I joined Facebook primarily to get a feel of what these precious young children were being exposed to. I treasured and valued my Sunday school children so much that I wanted to understand and be ready to counter false teachings and ungodliness with prayers and frank real-life talks.

Parents, when it comes to social media, be prepared to be on the same page with your children and possibly a couple of steps ahead with God's help and wisdom. Be sure you are walking your talk; otherwise you will lose them before you even start.

At the beginning of this chapter, I mentioned the need to build a "spiritual safety nest" around our children. Sometimes the best way to create this is through guided exposure. Be the one to introduce the embarrassing and touchy topics such as pre-marital sex, drugs, alcohol, pornography, and academic integrity before the world does or at least be ready with a counter answer. Be sure you are armed with the superior perspective of God's word and wisdom.

The devil and his agents are out there, perfecting their assignment to kill, steal and destroy. To deny this would be unwise. Here's what Jesus says in the bible: "The thief does not come except to steal, and to kill, and to destroy. I have come that they may have life, and that they may have it more abundantly." *John 10:10 NKJV*

Teaching his disciples to pray, he also said this:

"Our father in heaven, hallowed be Your name. Your kingdom come. Your will be done on earth as it is in heaven. ...... But deliver us from the evil one"
Luke 11: 2; 4c NKJV

We must ensure that these three assignments (Kill, Steal, and Destroy) of the thief (the Devil) pointed out by our Lord and Saviour Jesus Christ fail in the lives of our treasures. We must pray also that God delivers them from Satan, the evil one. Our children will go through their own share of troubles, temptations, trials and tribulations, but what they know and have learned through godly instructions, godly examples, correction and practical obedience will help them overcome. We must pray for them to be protected by the life-giving power that Jesus alone gives.

So how do we present and preserve our children as valuable treasures that heaven will accept?

1. Treat your children as treasures. We cannot hide our children from the world, but we can commit them into the hands of the One who is able to keep them from falling and ensure their safety. We must treasure and model God's love to them.

   "but lay up for yourselves treasures in heaven, where neither moth nor rust destroys and where thieves do not break

in and steal. For where your treasure is, there your heart will be also."
Matthew 6:20-21 NKJV

2. Pray for God's will to be done in the lives of your children. *"thy will be done on earth as it is in heaven."*
Matthew 6:10 NKJV

3. In addition to prayers, we need to practically guide them into fulfilling their destiny. We cannot afford to fail in the area of giving godly guidance and counseling. It is not by our power or might but by the Spirit of the Lord. We must depend on the Holy Spirit to lead us in giving the right and effective guidance in every situation. *"So he answered and said to me: "This is the word of the LORD to Zerubbabel: 'Not by might nor by power, but by My Spirit,' Says the LORD of hosts."*
Zechariah 4:6 NKJV

4. We must rely on Godly instructions, corrections and examples through the power of the Holy Spirit and consistently pray for them even after they leave home for education, work and eventually marriage.

5. We must intentionally pay attention to their friendship choices and other social interactions. We cannot control who they make friends with, but we can pray away every form of ungodly influence from their lives.

6. We must actively be our children's spiritual compasses. Jesus is the ultimate example of all Christian parents and children. But we must play our part and allow the Holy Spirit to work with the seeds we have planted in our children. How you value and protect your treasure will determine the quality of its output. We cannot afford to be careless.

7. There is also the place for godly discipline to keep children on track. To be effective, discipline should always be done in love. In my experience interacting with children, I found that those of them who eventually become "my buddies" are those that I was always very firm with. Children know when they get disciplined for wrong-doing and when it is done out of meanness. Do not be hesitant or "afraid" to discipline your children

as the need arise. They will appreciate it in years to come. God our Father disciplines us when we get out of line. His discipline is always to correct in love and to affirm that we are His children:

"And you have forgotten the exhortation which speaks to you as to sons: "My son, do not despise he chastening of the LORD, Nor be discouraged when you are rebuked by Him; For whom the LORD loves He chastens, And scourges every son whom He receives."
Hebrews 12:5-6 NKJV

Let us turn our focus on examples of children in the Bible whose parents' intentionality and walk with God positively impacted their lives.

Moses

Moses parents must have discerned or "heard from God" that there was a special call on his life. They took a great risk in going against Pharaoh's commands and refusing to give up their little boy to be killed. They intentionally devised a strategy to preserve his life. I believe this must have been an act of great faith in

God. His mother even ended up being paid to look after her own child - a reward for godly perception and bold actions. Here is how it happened:

> "And a man of the house of Levi went and took as wife a daughter of Levi. So the woman conceived and bore a son. And when she saw that he was a beautiful child, she hid him three months. But when she could no longer hide him, she took an ark of bulrushes for him, daubed it with asphalt and pitch, put the child in it, and laid it in the reeds by the river's bank. And his sister stood afar off, to know what would be done to him. Then the daughter of Pharaoh came down to bathe at the river. And her maidens walked along the riverside; and when she saw the ark among the reeds, she sent her maid to get it. And when she opened it, she saw the child, and behold, the baby wept. So she had compassion on him, and said, "This is one of the Hebrews' children." Then his sister said to Pharaoh's daughter, "Shall I go and call a nurse for you from the Hebrew women, that she may nurse the

child for you?" And Pharaoh's daughter said to her, "Go." So the maiden went and called the child's mother. Then Pharaoh's daughter said to her, "Take this child away and nurse him for me, and I will give you your wages." So the woman took the child and nursed him. And the child grew, and she brought him to Pharaoh's daughter, and he became her son. So she called his name Moses, saying, "Because I drew him out of the water".
Exodus 2:1-10 NKJV

Moses parents must have told him not to get carried away by the fact that he was the adopted son of Pharaoh's daughter. From all indications, Moses' mother used her position as Moses "baby-sitter" to instill in him Hebrew (godly) values that gave him the confidence to defy Egyptian culture and the choice to support his fellow Hebrews. Moses became the instrument God used to bring the Israelites out of slavery in Egypt, and he led them to the threshold of Canaan, the Promised Land.

We must be intentional in guiding the steps of our children into their God-given destinies.

Intentional guidance is one of the best legacies parents can give their children.

DANIEL AND HIS THREE FRIENDS

I believe that the parents of Daniel, Shadrack, Meshack and Abednego fall into the category of *"no-nonsense"* parents. Their parents must have impressed on their young minds Jewish values about eating and drinking to honour God. Their parents probably also had themselves rejected intoxicating drinks and food offered to idols. It must have come naturally for these four Hebrew boys to do the same when offered their daily portion of delicious meats and wine from king Nebuchadnezzar's palace.

> *"And the king appointed for them a daily provision of the king's `delicacies and of the wine which he drank, and three years of training for them, so that at the end of that time they might serve before the king. Now from among those of the sons of Judah were Daniel, Hananiah, Mishael, and Azariah. To them the chief of the eunuchs gave names: he gave Daniel the name*

Belteshazzar; to Hananiah, Shadrach; to Mishael, Meshach; and to Azariah, Abed-Nego. But Daniel purposed in his heart that he would not defile himself with the portion of the king's delicacies, nor with the wine which he drank; therefore he requested of the chief of the eunuchs that he might not defile himself. Now God had brought Daniel into the favor and goodwill of the chief of the eunuchs. "Please test your servants for ten days and let them give us vegetables to eat and water to drink. Thus the steward took away their portion of delicacies and the wine that they were to drink, and gave them vegetables. As for these four young men, God gave them knowledge and skill in all literature and wisdom; and Daniel had understanding in all visions and dreams."
Daniel 1:5-9, 12, 16-17 NKJV

Other than referring to Daniel, Shadrack, Meshack and Abednego as sons of Judah (descendants of Judah) no mention was made of their family life before their captivity in Babylon. Jesus Christ was also from the tribe of Judah. So, we can safely say that Daniel and his three friends had good "spiritual pedigree," which they lived up to. Like those in the lineage of Judah, they were obedient and served God faithfully. What was the outcome? God blessed these four young lads and they inherited a spirit of excellence and wisdom that empowered them to serve as the best advisors in the cabinet of King Nebuchadnezzar of the Persian kingdom. Daniel is recorded to have served in the cabinet of three kings in his generation Nebuchadnezzar, Belshazzar and Darius. We should make our children understand that God rewards consistent obedience and faithfulness.

Mordecai and Esther

When it comes to passing on Godly instructions to our children and living by example, Mordecai, the uncle of Esther, is a man every parent should aspire to be like and learn from. Through divine providence and guidance from her uncle, Esther was chosen by King Ahasuerus to become his queen in the place of Vashti. When Haman plotted the annihilation of all the Jews, Mordecai immediately led and proclaimed a fast for all the Jews to seek divine intervention from God. He did not mince words letting his niece know that her being queen would not exempt her from Haman's plot. This was the message he sent to her in the palace:

> *"And Mordecai told them to answer Esther: "Do not think in your heart that you will escape in the king's palace any more than all the other Jews. For if you remain completely silent at this time, relief and deliverance will arise for the Jews from another place, but you and your father's house will perish. Yet who knows whether you have come to the kingdom for such a time as this?"*
> *Esther 4:13-14 NKJV*

Mordecai could not have said it any clearer than that. He explicitly pointed out the looming danger to every Jew in Shushan, including Esther. He was very candid. This led Esther to boldly respond in obedience "….. and if I perish, I perish."

As parents, we too must be forthright with our children as the occasion warrants, regardless of their status. Being forthright and candid may well be what may be needed to help our children break off the mold and fulfil their destiny, as we see in the case of Esther. God put her in the position of a queen to bring deliverance to the Jews at that specific time in history. She fulfilled that assignment. As led by the Spirit of God, we too, need to give godly counsel to our children, even after they are grown up and have become independent adults.

Mrs. Naaman's Maid

This young Hebrew girl was taken from her family and home to Syria to work as a slave. She served as a maid to the wife of Naaman, the commander of the Syrian army. Despite her tragic circumstances, she still remembered her heritage taught to her by her parents or those who filled that role in her life. She knew the power of her God demonstrated in the prophets. It was with this confidence that she referred a leprosy stricken Naaman to Prophet Elisha in Samaria.

"And the Syrians had gone out on raids

and had brought back captive a young girl from the land of Israel. She waited on Naaman's wife. Then she said to her mistress, "If only my master were with the prophet who is in Samaria! For he would heal him of his leprosy. So he went down and dipped seven times in the Jordan, according to the saying of the man of God; and his flesh was restored like the flesh of a little child, and he was clean. And he returned to the man of God, he and all his aides, and came and stood before him; and he said, "Indeed, now I know that there is no God in all the earth, except in Israel; now therefore, please take a gift from your servant."
II Kings 5:2-3, 14-15 NKJV

What are you doing to build in your children confidence in God's power? We need to let our children know that there is nothing too difficult for God. There is no situation He cannot reverse or make better. We must talk about the great things God has done in our lives and in the lives of others. Our children need to know our testimonies, so their faith in God can become strong. With that knowledge, they can rely on God when they are alone or when "life happens," and they go through challenging times. Instead of living in despair, a slave girl "evangelized" a top-ranking military man!

After his healing by prophet Elisha in Samaria, Naaman placed his faith in the God of Israel. He even took some of the sand from Samaria back with to Syria. This is symbolic of his continued worship of the God who healed him.

> *So Naaman said, "Then, if not, please let your servant be given two mule-loads of earth; for your servant will no longer offer either burnt offering or sacrifice to other gods, but to the LORD."*
> *II Kings 5:17 NKJV*

Prayer Seed

Father, I ask for grace to be intentional in training my children. May my lifestyle be consistent with the values I seek to instill in my children. May they be obedient and love your ways. Shield them from the evil one and his tricks. Give them the wisdom and courage to make the right choices, even when it is difficult. May they not come under destructive peer pressure.

When feeling all alone or facing challenges, may the Holy Spirit remind them of your love for them and that you are always with them and will give them the power and wisdom to overcome. I ask all these in Jesus mighty name. Amen!

Scripture Boost

"And do not lead us into temptation but deliver us from the evil one. For Yours is the kingdom and the power and the glory forever. Amen."
Matthew 6:13 NKJV

"Children, obey your parents in the Lord, for this is right. And you, fathers, do not provoke your children to wrath, but bring them up in the training and admonition of the Lord".
Ephesians 6:1, 4 NKJV

"And the LORD, He is the One who goes before you. He will be with you, He will not leave you nor forsake you; do not fear nor be dismayed."
Deuteronomy 31:8 NKJV

My Action Journal

From today, with God's help, I will begin to:

1.

2.

3.

5/Five

Could it Have Had a Different Ending?

What lessons can we learn from the parents spotlighted from the bible? We know that each of them played an active role in motivating and supporting their children into fulfilling their God-assigned roles and destinies.

Our children are part of the earthly treasures we must aim at storing up in heaven. If some of these parents had disobeyed direct instructions from God or timely prompting from the Holy Spirit to take certain actions, the outcome would have been different for the lives of their children, and I dare say human history.

On the other hand, for parents who failed to give godly instructions or demonstrate a godly lifestyle of obedience to their children, there were far-reaching consequences. The disobedience of those parents affected the destinies of their children in more ways than we can imagine.

Eli the Priest

Eli did not train his children in godly obedience, and he ignored God's instruction to discipline his sons. Though Eli reprimanded his sons when he learned of their vile actions, God expected a better response from Eli. For example, Eli could have removed his sons from serving in the temple to avoid dishonoring God's offerings. As a result of his lack of action, the dishonorable behavior of Eli's sons became an evil God inputted on Eli's entire family line and not just on his sons.

A curse was pronounced on Eli's sons and his family was cut off from priesthood.

> *"Now Eli was very old; and he heard everything his sons did to all Israel, and how*

they lay with the women who assembled at the door of the tabernacle of meeting. Why do you kick at My sacrifice and My offering which I have commanded in My dwelling place, and honor your sons more than Me, to make yourselves fat with the best of all the offerings of Israel My people?' Behold, the days are coming that I will cut off your arm and the arm of your father's house, so that there will not be an old man in your house."
I Samuel 2:22, 29, 31 NKJV

"And therefore I have sworn to the house of Eli that the iniquity of Eli's house shall not be atoned for by sacrifice or offering forever."
I Samuel 3:14 NKJV

"Then the man said to Eli, "I am he who came from the battle. And I fled today from the battle line." And he said, "What happened, my son?" So the messenger answered and said, "Israel has fled before the Philistines, and there has been a great slaughter among the people. Also your two sons, Hophni and Phinehas, are dead;

and the ark of God has been captured." Then it happened, when he made mention of the ark of God, that Eli fell off the seat backward by the side of the gate; and his neck was broken and he died, for the man was old and heavy. And he had judged Israel forty years."
I Samuel 4:16-18 NKJV

On the same day Eli and his sons died, the Ark of Covenant was also captured. Eli's actions or lack thereof, impacted the entire nation of Israel. God's presence was removed from them. This was a huge blow to the Israelites, whose confidence to face the enemies that surrounded them was on the physical presence of the Ark of Covenant. It symbolized God's presence amongst them.

Eli's entire bloodline and legacy were wiped out on earth, and by inference, Eli lost storing treasures in heaven. What other consequences can be graver and more far-reaching than these?

Eli may have probably been too "busy" doing God's work that he failed to move in prayer and repentance for his children. Parents, should not tolerate their children treating the things of God with levity. Our children must be taught to avoid making jokes about spiritual things like unbelievers do today, knowing that the consequences can be devastating with curses on generations yet unborn. Let us, therefore, give ourselves to intentional discipline and make continual intercession for our children.

KING SAUL

King Saul is another example where God rejected a man and cut off his entire lineage from the throne of Israel on account of his sin. King Saul disobeyed God and his godly son, Jonathan, was affected by the consequences of God's rejection of his father.

> *"But Samuel said to Saul, "I will not return with you, for you have rejected the word of the LORD, and the LORD has rejected you from being king over Israel." So Samuel said to him, "The LORD has torn the kingdom of Israel from you today, and has given it to a neighbor of yours, who is better than you." I Samuel 15:26, 28 NKJV*

Saul and his son, Jonathan, were both killed violently in battle. Jonathan probably might have become king if the script was played differently by his father.

Mr. & Mrs. Manoah - Samson's Parents

God clearly told the parents of Samson how he was to be raised on account of His purpose for Samson's life. Samson was to be "a Nazarite to God from the womb," set apart completely for God's use. There are rules for being a Nazarite, and God thoroughly explained those rules to Manoah and his wife before Samson was born. For example, Manoah and Samson's mother were to abstain from anything unclean, and Samson's hair must never be cut:

> *"Now therefore, please be careful not to drink wine or similar drink, and not to eat anything unclean. For behold, you shall conceive and bear a son. And no razor shall come upon his head, for the child shall be a Nazirite to God from the womb; and he shall begin to deliver Israel out of the hand of the Philistines."*
> *Judges 13:4-5 NKJV*

Partial obedience to God's instruction can greatly harm our children. The Angel of the Lord was explicit in explaining the requirements to the Manoahs on his second visit, and their initial response was very commendable. They offered a burnt sacrifice to God in appreciation of His apparent goodness to their family. It would later appear that they probably did not follow through with all the implied requirements for raising a Nazarite child. I believe Samson's struggle in his affairs with women and the eventual outcome of his life can be attributed to his parents indulging him at the expense of God's instructions.

God does not have to necessarily spell out every detail of His instructions or plans for us. As believers, we must learn to "read between the lines." No razor was to touch Samson's head, and he was to abstain from strong drink (alcohol). By extension, Samson should have also been counseled to abstain from getting himself a heathen wife or maybe to remain celibate as a Nazarite. However, his parents failed to caution him against these when he desired to marry Delilah, a Philistine woman.

In my opinion, Samson's parents (not knowing how God wanted to achieve his plan of delivering Israel from the Philistine oppression) should have stood their ground when he insisted on marrying Delilah. Their action (without knowing what we now know from scripture) was indulging. As a result of his own decisions, Samson's life ended tragically though God's sovereign purpose for Israel was still fulfilled. We must not be afraid to caution and advise our adult children when we are convinced they want to take an ungodly action. Though Samson destroyed Israel's Philistine enemies, he died with the enemies of God. That could not have been God's plan for him though. God listened to his prayer of "repentance" and defended the integrity of His word and person in the end.

In order to leave a godly heritage for our children, we must learn to be firm when our children attempt to stray from obedience to God and let them know the consequences of their intended actions. As we continue to pray for them, we must know when to put our feet down and know when our no must stay and remain so.

King David

King David made a colossal error of judgement by committing adultery, followed by murder to cover things up. The consequences were far-reaching and should serve as a "teachable moment" for all parents. Careless or thoughtless actions can destroy our families. As a result of David's actions and God's judgement, incest, rebellion and murder were experienced in his family. These evil acts were committed by David's own children. Though God was merciful and forgave David for his actions after he repented, the consequences of his actions lingered on. It was only by the providence and predestination of God that Jesus Christ our Lord came from the line of David to put an end to the curse pronounced in this passage:

> *"Then Nathan said to David, "You are the man! Thus says the LORD God of Israel: 'I anointed you king over Israel, and I delivered you from the hand of Saul. I gave you your master's house and your master's wives into your keeping, and gave you the house of Israel and Judah. And if that had*

> been too little, I also would have given you much more! Why have you despised the commandment of the LORD, to do evil in His sight? You have killed Uriah the Hittite with the sword; you have taken his wife to be your wife, and have killed him with the sword of the people of Ammon. Now therefore, the sword shall never depart from your house, because you have despised Me, and have taken the wife of Uriah the Hittite to be your wife.' Thus says the LORD: 'Behold, I will raise up adversity against you from your own house; and I will take your wives before your eyes and give them to your neighbor, and he shall lie with your wives in the sight of this sun. For you did it secretly, but I will do this thing before all Israel, before the sun.
> II Samuel 12:7-12 NKJV

Here are some of the outcomes of the above pronouncement against David:

> "After this Absalom the son of David had a lovely sister, whose name was Tamar; and Amnon the son of David loved her. Amnon was so distressed over his sister Tamar that

he became sick; for she was a virgin. And it was improper for Amnon to do anything to her. And he said to him, "Why are you, the king's son, becoming thinner day after day? Will you not tell me?" Amnon said to him, "I love Tamar, my brother Absalom's sister." So Jonadab said to him, "Lie down on your bed and pretend to be ill. And when your father comes to see you, say to him, 'Please let my sister Tamar come and give me food, and prepare the food in my sight, that I may see it and eat it from her hand.' "Then Amnon lay down and pretended to be ill; and when the king came to see him, Amnon said to the king, "Please let Tamar my sister come and make a couple of cakes for me in my sight, that I may eat from her hand." And David sent home to Tamar, saying, "Now go to your brother Amnon's house, and prepare food for him." So Tamar went to her brother Amnon's house; and he was lying down. Then she took flour and kneaded it, made cakes in his sight, and baked the cakes. And she took the pan and placed them out before him, but he refused to eat. Then

Amnon said, "Have everyone go out from me." And they all went out from him. Then Amnon said to Tamar, "Bring the food into the bedroom, that I may eat from your hand." And Tamar took the cakes which she had made, and brought them to Amnon her brother in the bedroom. Now when she had brought them to him to eat, he took hold of her and said to her, "Come, lie with me, my sister." But she answered him, "No, my brother, do not force me, for no such thing should be done in Israel. Do not do this disgraceful thing! And I, where could I take my shame? And as for you, you would be like one of the fools in Israel. Now therefore, please speak to the king; for he will not withhold me from you." However, he would not heed her voice; and being stronger than she, he forced her and lay with her. Then Amnon hated her exceedingly, so that the hatred with which he hated her was greater than the love with which he had loved her. And Amnon said to her, "Arise, be gone!" So she said to him, "No, indeed! This evil of sending me away is worse than the other that you did

to me." But he would not listen to her. Then he called his servant who attended him, and said, "Here! Put this woman out, away from me, and bolt the door behind her." Now she had on a robe of many colors, for the king's virgin daughters wore such apparel. And his servant put her out and bolted the door behind her. Then Tamar put ashes on her head, and tore her robe of many colors that was on her, and laid her hand on her head and went away crying bitterly. And Absalom her brother said to her, "Has Amnon your brother been with you? But now hold your peace, my sister. He is your brother; do not take this thing to heart." So Tamar remained desolate in her brother Absalom's house. But when King David heard of all these things, he was very angry. And Absalom spoke to his brother Amnon neither good nor bad. For Absalom hated Amnon, because he had forced his sister Tamar."
II Samuel 13:1-2, 4-22 NKJV

Hatred, bitterness and unforgiveness toward his half-brother led Absalom to devise a murderous plan which he tactfully executed. David, his father, committed murder to cover up adultery. Years later, his son Absalom committed murder to avenge a rape/incest. This is clearly a bad flow. Absalom later died a tragic death when his head was caught between the branches of trees while fleeing from his father's army after his rebellion. It takes the divine mercy of God to stop such evil flow from a family lineage.

Prayer Seed

Dear Lord, I ask that you give me the grace to instill godly discipline in my children and that their hearts be inclined towards obedience. I uproot every seed of disobedience from the hearts of my children. In Jesus mighty name, Amen.

Father may my children not become collateral damage for my errors. I repent from all my wrong attitudes and sins. Please have mercy on me and forgive me. I pray that the blood of Jesus Christ speaks mercy over my lineage, may it cleanse generational sins and break all curses there may be. Thank you, Lord, for deliverance and grace to live free and secure in your love and mercies. Amen.

Scripture Boost

> *"So Samuel said: "Has the LORD as great delight in burnt offerings and sacrifices, As in obeying the voice of the LORD? Behold, to obey is better than sacrifice, And to heed than the fat of rams."*
> *I Samuel 15:11-2 NKJV*

"My son, do not despise the chastening of the LORD, Nor detest His correction; For whom the LORD loves He corrects, Just as a father the son in whom he delights."
Proverbs 3:11-12 NKJV

If we say we have no sins, we deceive ourselves, and the truth is not in us. If we confess our sins, He is faithful and just to forgive us our sins and to cleanse us from all unrighteousness.
1 John 1:8-9 NKJV

"For judgment is without mercy to the one who has shown no mercy. Mercy triumphs over judgment."
James 2:13 NKJV

My Action Journal

From today, with God's help, I will begin to:

1.

2.

3.

6/Six

MAKE YOUR ARROWS SHARP

The Bible describes children as "arrows."

"Like arrows in the hands of a warrior; So are the children of one's youth"
Psalm 127:4 NKJV

In ancient days, arrows were an important part of a nation's armory. They were also used by hunters and for personal protection. God wants our children to be strong and well-directed in life. An arrow cannot function effectively if it is blunt. In that condition, it is a useless arrow. How can an arrow be effective for its intended use?

1. The tip must be well sharpened.

2. The person throwing the arrow must focus on the target in a game or in battle.

Parents are primarily responsible for the direction the arrow is sent and the purpose for which it is being sent. How do we ensure that our children are spiritually sharp, and how do we as parents remain focused to ensure our children are properly directed in order to fulfill destiny?

> *"For a good tree does not bear bad fruit, nor does a bad tree bear good fruit. For every tree is known by its own fruit. For men do not gather figs from thorns, nor do they gather grapes from a bramble bush. A good man out of the good treasure of his heart brings forth good; and an evil man out of the evil treasure of his heart brings forth evil. For out of the abundance of the heart his mouth speaks."*
> *Luke 6:43-45 NKJV*

Parents must not misdirect their children in any way. We must equip them mentally, physically, socially and ensure that they are properly instructed in the word of God. We must aim at producing well balanced and "total children." Your lifestyle is usually a pointer to the direction your children are likely to follow as they grow and mature. Parents, we must keep examining ourselves to see if we are on course and are walking our spiritual and moral talk to our children. The above scripture is clear. We cannot produce or reproduce what is not in us. We cannot give what we do not have.

Grace for Parenting

By the grace of God, there are exceptions to every rule. For those parents who may not have had it all together, simply by God's mercies and grace, your children can turn out positively different and avoid replicating the mistakes you may have made. They will become more than your better versions. Parents need to stay connected with God in prayer. As they do so, in total dependence on the grace which God alone supplies, they will be able to model the qualities they want to see in their children.

God's expectations of parents remain the same, even in a time where moral standards appear to be in an all-time low. We owe it to ourselves and our children to stand strong just as Paul says, "... and having done all, to stand" Ephesians 6:13c NKJV.

Our lives in the open and in private must be consistently what we can commend to our children as examples for them to follow.

How then can we make our children like sharp arrows? We must depend on God.

> "Unless the LORD builds the house, They labor in vain who build it; Unless the LORD guards the city, The watchman stays awake in vain. It is vain for you to rise up early, To sit up late, To eat the bread of sorrows; For so He gives His beloved sleep. Behold, children are a heritage from the LORD, The fruit of the womb is a reward. Like arrows in the hand of a warrior, So are the children of one's youth. Happy is the man who has his quiver full of them; They shall not be ashamed But shall speak with their enemies in the gate."
> Psalms 127:1-5 NKJV

The outcome of our parenting effort is totally

dependent on God. There are no superstar parents. We must prayerfully and purposefully call on God for help, pulling from the resources He has made available to us.

God is the only super parent there is. We must learn to commit every stage of our children's development to Him. We have a role to play in how we live and how we raise our children, but it is God alone that can ensure that our children turn out well.

God's standard of discipline as an expression of love is fast becoming outdated. We need to recognise that the alternative lifestyles promoted today are a deceptive tool of the devil to ultimately wipe out humanity. So, let us fight together for our children and for a generation yet unborn and ensure that our arrows are sharp, properly directed, and secure in our hands. Let us pray that the minds of our children will not get ensnared by all the appealing deceptive schemes of the devil.

The Bible and indeed human history have revealed that God deals with his children with eternity in mind. He takes a long-term position on all things, whether good or bad. We have seen from biblical examples that our good and bad actions or inactions can have long term consequences that extend beyond us. We are made in the image of God and are admonished to be like Him. We must, therefore, live with eternity in mind. We must become deeply conscious that what we do (or fail to do in some cases...) will affect our children and generations after us.

A family as consistently depicted in the Bible, based on God's eternal model is made up of a mother who is genetically female and a father who is genetically male together with the children that He chooses to bless them with.

> *"So God created man in His own image; in the image of God He created him; male and female He created them."*
> Genesis 1:27 NKJV

> *"He created them male and female, and blessed them and called them Mankind in the day they were created."*
> Genesis 5:2 NKJV

We need to teach our children the biblical truth about the composition of a family.

So, I leave you with these scriptures to motivate you to always be conscious that your today affects your tomorrow and those of your children and unborn generations. Be careful and mindful therefore, so you can partake of God's mercies and faithfulness.

> "Therefore know that the LORD your God, He is God, the faithful God who keeps covenant and mercy for a thousand generations with those who love Him and keep His commandments."
> Deuteronomy 7:9 NKJV

> "keeping mercy for thousands, forgiving iniquity and transgression and sin, by no means clearing the guilty, visiting the iniquity of the fathers upon the children and the children's children to the third and the fourth generation"
> Exodus 34:7 NKJV

May our actions today bring eternal blessings to our children. May our children not be ashamed to carry on where we stopped, and may they be empowered to improve on the things we have done. May their reflections on our ways after we are gone draw them closer to God in faith, love and service. The future of the Church universal and of all nations are dependent on how we raise our children today. One child well-raised is the foundation of an entire godly generation for tomorrow.

Prayer Seed

I receive God's grace to live in obedience. May my life be an example of godly standards for my children to follow. May my life not bring shame and sorrow on my seed. I receive wisdom to guide my children in the direction that God has ordained for them. May I not lead my children into error. In Jesus mighty name I pray, Amen.

Scripture Boost

"Then Manoah prayed to the LORD, and said, "O my Lord, please let the Man of God whom You sent come to us again and teach us what we shall do for the child who will be born." And God listened to the voice of Manoah, and the Angel of God came to the woman again as she was sitting in the field; but Manoah her husband was not with her. Manoah said, "Now let Your words come to pass! What will be the boy's rule of life, and his work?" So the Angel of the LORD said to Manoah, "Of all that I said to the woman let her be careful. She may not eat anything that

comes from the vine, nor may she drink wine or similar drink, nor eat anything unclean. All that I commanded her let her observe."
Judges 13:8-9, 12-14 NKJV

"In those days they shall say no more: 'The fathers have eaten sour grapes, And the children's teeth are set on edge.' But every one shall die for his own iniquity; every man who eats the sour grapes, his teeth shall be set on edge."
Jeremiah 31:29-30 NKJV

My Action Journal

From today, with God's help, I will begin to:

1.

2.

3.

7/Seven

Reflections

When my children were growing up, I taught them to pray the following scriptures:

> "In those days they shall say no more: 'The fathers have eaten sour grapes, And the children's teeth are set on edge.' But everyone shall die for his own iniquity; every man who eats the sour grapes, his teeth shall be set on edge."
> Jeremiah 31:29-30 NKJV

> "What do you mean when you use this proverb concerning the land of Israel, saying: 'The fathers have eaten sour grapes, And the children's teeth are set on edge'? As I live," says the Lord GOD, "you

shall no longer use this proverb in Israel. "Behold, all souls are Mine; The soul of the father as well as the soul of the son is Mine; The soul who sins shall die."
Ezekiel 18:2-4 NKJV

I taught my children to pray these prayers because I realized that God had lavished His mercies on me. The understanding God gave me about my background imposed on me the responsibility to ensure that my children never went through the paths I had to tread. I had to fight the generational battle not only for myself but for my children and generations to come.

As parents, we must prayerfully ask God to reveal to us issues there may be in our past, we need to deal with so that our children can live and fulfil their destinies unhindered.

Thanks be to God for His mercies and the dispensation of grace that we now enjoy. I encourage all parents to pray these scriptures over their children regardless of what you believe your standing is with God.

May the destinies of our children not be

set on edge on account of our sins and other misdeeds. Gehazi, prophet Elisha's servant was portrayed in the scriptures as a greedy person. Elisha had refused to accept gratification from Naaman after he was healed of leprosy. Gehazi thereafter ran after Naaman to collect some of the gift items he had offered to Elisha. Elisha witnessed the incident "in the spirit." When confronted, Gehazi lied about where he had been. Elisha therefore pronounced a curse on him that affected him and his descendants.

> "Therefore the leprosy of Naaman shall cling to you and your descendants forever." And he went out from his presence leprous, as white as snow."
> II Kings 5:27 NKJV

By implication, Gehazi's lineage was cut off from serving as ministers of God. Leprosy was considered an unclean disease, and therefore, those who suffer from it were prevented from entering the temple of God to worship or to serve. They were also social outcasts. (Leviticus 13 & 14).

We have a choice on the type of legacy

we leave our children. May we not leave a "leprous inheritance" to generations coming after us because of our actions.

> *"Whoever causes one of these little ones who believes in me to sin, it would be better for him if a millstone were hung around his neck, and he were drowned in the depth of the sea."*
> *Matthew 18:6 NKJV*

This warning from our Lord Jesus himself should be taken literally, so we do not lose sight of the responsibility to nurture our young ones and all coming after us as we have grace and opportunity.

We need to be careful about how we live, so we do not end up leaving the next generation spiritual and economic liabilities. We must not make them pay for sins or actions, not their own.

I leave you a thought-provoking scripture and urge you to make life-enhancing choices so your children can live life when you have gone to meet with the Lord:

MY ACTION JOURNAL

From today, with God's help, I will begin to:

1.

2.

3.

PRESERVING YOUR NEXT GENERATION

"I call heaven and earth as witnesses today against you, that I have set before you life and death, blessing and cursing; therefore choose life, that both **you and your descendants may live;"**
Deuteronomy 30:19 NKJV

Prayer Seed

Dear reader, please pray for yourself regarding what the Holy Spirit may have convicted you about or what that still small voice kept echoing as you were reading this chapter:

_____

_____

Scripture Boost

"And if it seems evil to you to serve the LORD, choose for yourselves this day whom you will serve, whether the gods which your fathers served that were on the other side of the River, or the gods of the Amorites, in whose land you dwell. But as for me and my house, we will serve the LORD."
Joshua 24:15 NKJV

8/Eight

Bringing it Closer

I was not very intentional with my parenting when raising my two sons. My husband was more intentional in terms of their education and career choices. I took care of the spiritual side of things. We both made mistakes that could have had undesirable consequences on their future but for the mercies of God.

One lesson I learned in my years of ministry is not to let slide by any opportunity God brings you to impact the life of a child, especially those not yours biologically. One life in God's reckoning is a generation. Therefore, do not withhold a good deed you can do for someone today because you are not guaranteed a repeat of the opportunity. To delay or withhold can cause us to lose a generational impact or blessing. God will surely hold us accountable. I embraced some opportunities that came my way and some I wasted following my flesh and not God's Spirit. I believe I have received God's forgiveness and mercy, having prayed and confessed those sins as convicted by the Spirit of God.

Parents, I know we sometimes have legitimate pressures in the course of everyday living. There is the tendency to vent some of those pressures on our children. They know whenever we do that, and they question mostly silently. If this goes unchecked, we stand the risk of losing our "credibility" as parents. So, be intentionally sensitive to your feelings and those of your children. Learn to give those pressures to God and let Jesus carry the burdens, whatever they may be. Jesus cares much more than we can ever know.

"Casting all your care upon Him, for He cares for you."

I Peter 5:7 NKJV

"Come to Me, all you who labor and are heavy laden, and I will give you rest. Take My yoke upon you and learn from Me, for I am gentle and lowly in heart, and you will find rest for your souls. For My yoke is easy and My burden is light."
Matthew 11:28-30 NKJV

Part of my prayers at a stage in my life was for God to give me a second chance to correct some of the mistakes I believed I made. I still find myself praying this prayer occasionally. I believe both my sons are living within their God-ordained destinies. The glory for that belongs to God. God delivered me from all my fears as I prayed and will keep praying. I remember attending the graduation ceremony of one of my sons, and at the reception held by the church for their members who graduated, the pastor's wife pulled me aside and told me some of the roles my son played in the church and services he contributed to the community.

I was overwhelmed with joy, and tears rolled down my cheeks uncontrollably. God sent her to me to let me know beyond a shadow of a doubt that He had not only answered my prayers but that I had nothing to worry about all those years because He had been by his side all along, guiding his every step.

I write this book as a grandmother of two, and deep inside I believe God has given me an opportunity to correct some of my mistakes. As a silent observer, I say thank you, God, for some of the things I see. For others, I pray for the perfect timing to say a word in godly wisdom to put things in proper perspective. I seal these testimonies with praise and the overcoming blood of Jesus Christ.

It is with deep humility that I say these very personal things. Dear reader, I want you to know and believe that it is only God Almighty who crowns all our parenting efforts with blessings and good success. Rest assured also that there are no errors we make as parents that God cannot forgive, redeem us and give us a brand-new start.

I am glad that God allowed me to write this book at this time. I lost the handwritten manuscript of the first book I attempted to write while my boys were still teenagers. I had titled it "Boys to Men." What I lost on paper God is writing for me real-time. If I was to rewrite the book (and I pray I do), I have real-life materials to include not only from my sons' lives but from the lives of other boys I have watched grow into fine and god-fearing young men, husbands and fathers.

We need to make prayer investments in our children. Regardless of the challenges we encounter, I assure you that the outcome will glorify God if we do not give up – on ourselves and our children. I believe God wants me to share this: I once prayed to God to give my younger son a second chance when he missed writing a critical examination on account of a mix-up with the time. It was totally my mistake. Did God answer, yes with a miracle that still gives me the shivers. By late afternoon of the same day, the very same examination that he missed writing on account of my mistake was cancelled in the entire region on account of some administrative lapses by the exam board! I cannot stop thanking God for His mercies.

Be a next-generation parent, focus on eternity and be intentional in everything you do.

EPILOGUE

1

GENERATIONAL BLESSINGS

I command the blessing of Yahweh, our heavenly father over your seeds.

- May they never be misdirected arrows.
- May they stay rooted in the Savior's hands.
- May the life of Yeshua HaMashiach fill their souls.
- May the light of God's love glow from them to stop the gloom of darkness in their world.
- May the Sword of the Spirit never drop from their hands.
- May they daily draw strength and wisdom from God the Father.
- May their souls never be corrupted by the decay and deception all around them.

- May they be taught by the Lord and so have great peace all the days of their lives.
- May their lives be filed with the presence of the Holy Spirit.
- May they be insulated in coverings of the Blood of the Lamb of God and the burning fire of the Holy Ghost to remain aglow and live in divine safety.
- May their strengths never wane, may their courage never fail.
- May they find true counsel and support in their times of trouble.
- May they always hear and recognise the Good Shepherd's voice.
- May He lead them into safe and fruitful pastures.
- May they never follow the counsel of the wicked, stand in the way of sinners or sit on the seat of mockers, may they delight in the word and instructions of God and thus become trees planted by rivers of water, yielding their fruits in season and may they

remain fruitful and never wither.

- May it be unto them as it is written for them in The Books of heaven, so they fulfil their respective destinies.

- May they transform their world into pictures and foretaste of heaven.

- May they remain engraved in the palm of God's hands and their names remain in the Lamb's Book of Life.

- May they receive the royal welcome of faithful servants and partake of their Father's eternal joy. Amen.

My dear reader, may you rejoice in the fruit of your seed as the spirit and truth of Proverbs 22:16 become your testimony regarding your seed:

"Train up a (your) child the way he should go, when he is old he will not depart from it."

So, shall it be in Jesus mighty name.
Amen.

2

Keep it Burning and Pass it on . . .

What do you have to give?
What will you leave behind?
What will you leave for them?
What will you give your Seed?

You can command blessings,
Blessings over your seed.
Live your life so you can leave blessings,
A blessed heritage for your seed.

The things you do they see,
The words you speak they hear.
The way you tread they ponder,
Your light they need to see.

Guide them to the Savior's feet,
Guide their feet to the Master.
Guide their hearts to the Savior,
Guide them to trust in God.

Show and teach them to love,
Love the Lord their God.

Alero Nwana

Show and teach them to serve,
Serve the Lord their God.

Let your words show them,
Let your actions tell them.
Let your ways compel them,
That Jesus is the only Way.

There's only one truth to tell,
Only one way to show.
Only one path to tread,
The way of Jesus, Savior and Lord!

The legacies going into eternity,
The crowns to wear in heaven.
Hearing God's voice say, "well done,"
Are generations you've banked in Heaven.

Seeds and lives you've planted in the Lord,
Arrows you've directed and rooted in the Savior's hands.
Souls you've ignited with the Word of God,
Are generations next in line to keep it burning!

3

Song: Jesus Cares

"Casting all your cares upon Him, for He cares for you." (1 Peter 5:7)

Lyrics: Alero Nwana; Music: Chukwunonso Diali

Jesus my Lord is good,
Jesus my Lord is kind.
Jesus my Lord is loving,
Jesus, He cares for me.
Jesus cares!

Jesus my Lord is humble,
Jesus my Lord is true.
Jesus my Lord is caring,
Jesus, He cares for you.
Jesus cares!

Jesus my Lord is gentle,
Jesus my Lord is strong.
Jesus my Lord is forgiving,

ALERO NWANA

Jesus, He cares for us.
Jesus cares!

Jesus my Lord is merciful,
Jesus my Lord is faithful.
Jesus my Lord is gracious,
Jesus, He cares for all.
Jesus cares!

Jesus, He cares for me,
Jesus, He cares for you.
Jesus, He cares for us.
Jesus, He cares for all!
Jesus cares, yes, He cares!

Jesus Cares

4

Eternal Investment: Pray for Your Children

> *"But thus says the Lord: "Even the captives of the mighty shall be taken away, And the prey of the terrible delivered; For I will contend with him who contend with you, And I will save your children."*
> *Isaiah 49:25 NKJV*

> *"Children, obey your parents in all things, for this is well pleasing to the Lord. Fathers, do not provoke your children, lest they become discouraged."*
> *Colossians 3:20-21 NKJV*

Father, I stand on your promise in Isaiah 49:25 that you will save my children. I ask for the grace not to provoke or exasperate them as I strive to raise them to be godly and obedient children.

1. I thank you, Lord, because you are my father and you care for my children and love and them.

2. I believe your word is true, is active, alive and sharper than any double-edged sword.

3. I thank you for blessing me with children and giving me the grace to care for them.

4. I ask that you forgive all my sins and those of my children and family. I receive mercy and forgiveness today in Jesus mighty name.

5. Your Word says you are able to deliver and save those who trust in you. Therefore I stand to pray for my children and ask that you deliver them from every form of bondage and addiction.

6. I pray that you reverse every medical condition that has been pronounced over any of my children. I pray that you heal and deliver them from every limitation they are currently dealing with. Heal their minds, souls and bodies.

7. I pray that you deliver my children from every bondage they are under due to evil words spoken over them and on account of the circumstances of their birth and ungodly family inheritance.

8. I thank you, God, that my children shall continue to walk in divine obedience, divine instruction and direction. Thank you that all my children are taught of the Lord, and they enjoy great peace.
Isaiah 54:13 NKJV

9. I pray away from my children every form of ungodly influence in any environment they are in, in the name of Jesus Christ.

10. I receive divine grace and wisdom to care for my children. I shall not become weary or discouraged in Jesus name.

11. My children shall glorify God in all their ways all the days of their lives and shall be examples of godliness and obedience in Jesus mighty name. "Train up a child the way he should go, when he grows up he will not depart from it."
Proverbs 22:6 NKJV

12. Father in the name of Jesus, Christ I pray that my children will be obedient, I break away from them the spirit of the horse. They shall not be heady but shall have divine

understanding, perception and wisdom. Do not be like the horse or like the mule, Which have no understanding, Which must be harnessed with bit and bridle, Else they will not come near you.
Psams 32:9 NKJV

13. I raise the standard of the powerful name of Jesus Christ against every affliction and sickness of the body mind and soul in the lives of my children and I command them to leave now and never return. "that at the name of Jesus every knee should bow, of those in heaven, and of those on earth, and of those under the earth"
Philippians 2:10 NKJV

14. My children shall not walk in the counsel of the wicked, nor stand in the way of sinners nor sit on the seat of scoffers. They shall delight in the law of the Lord.
Psalm 1:1-2 NKJV

15. My children and I, my entire household shall serve the Lord.
Joshua 24:15 NKJV

16. Father may my children never live their lives in lack. Provide for them all they need to know, love and serve you. "Use your powerful arm and rescue me from the hands of mere humans whose world won't last. You provide food for those you love. Their children have plenty, and their grandchildren will have more than enough."
Psalms 17:14 CEV

"I have been young, and now am old; Yet I have never seen the righteous forsaken, Nor his descendants begging bread."
Psalm 37:25 NKJV

17. May my children never come under the deception of the devil. May their minds not be crowded by the love of this world and its offerings that they forget that God exists and that He is sovereign over affairs of mankind.

"When all that generation had been gathered to their fathers, another generation arose after them who did not know the LORD nor the work which He had done for Israel."
Judges 2:10 NKJV

18. May my children not come under the spirit of deception. May they never accept the lies of the enemy but stand on the truth of God's word. May they never come under the evil influence of those "who exchanged the truth of God for a lie..."
Romans 1:25a NKJV

19. *My children shall manifest the fullness of the fruit of the Spirit, love joy, peace, patience, kindness, faithfulness, humility and self-control in every area of their lives.*
Galatians 5:23 NKJV

20. Father release the spirit of prophesy over my sons and daughters. May they be your willing instruments of instructions and transformation in their generation; may they see things that are hidden in plain sight in Jesus mighty name.

   "And it shall come to pass afterward That I will pour my out my Spirit on all flesh; Your sons and your daughters shall prophesy, ... Your young men shall see visions."
   Joel 2:28 NKJV

21. I thank you, Lord, for answering my prayers and defending your word concerning my children. May your word that is spirit and life be alive in my children in Jesus mighty name. Amen.

www.ingramcontent.com/pod-product-compliance
Lightning Source LLC
Chambersburg PA
CBHW071701040426
42446CB00011B/1867